MODERN

Booties for Baby

by Kristi Simpson

Kick up some cuteness with crochet booties that are packed with modern details. Baby girls and boys will be fashion stars in these slippers, boots, and other styles of footwear.

LEISURE ARTS, INC.
Maumelle, Arkansas

Casual Boots

EASY

SHOPPING LIST

Yarn (Medium Weight) MEDIUM 4

- ☐ Green - 85 yards (77.5 meters)
- ☐ Tan - 15 yards (13.5 meters)

Crochet Hook

- ☐ Size F (3.75 mm)
  or size needed for gauge

Additional Supplies

- ☐ Split ring marker or scrap yarn
- ☐ 1" (25 mm) Button - 2
- ☐ Sewing needle and thread

SIZE INFORMATION

Small: 2" wide x 3" long
(5 cm x 7.5 cm)

Medium: 2" wide x 3½" long
(5 cm x 9 cm)

Size Note: We have printed the instructions for the sizes in different colors to make it easier for you to find:

- Size Small in Blue
- Size Medium in Pink

Instructions in Black apply to both sizes.

GAUGE INFORMATION

Gauge Swatch: 2" wide x 3{3½}" long
[5 cm x 7.5{9} cm]

Work same as Sole.

STITCH GUIDE

SINGLE CROCHET 2 TOGETHER
(abbreviated sc2tog)

Pull up a loop in each of next 2 sts, YO and draw through all 3 loops on hook **(counts as one sc)**.

DOUBLE CROCHET 2 TOGETHER
(abbreviated dc2tog)
(uses next 2 sts)

★ YO, insert hook in **next** st, YO and pull up a loop, YO and draw through 2 loops on hook; repeat from ★ once **more**, YO and draw through all 3 loops on hook **(counts as one dc)**.

FRONT POST DOUBLE CROCHET
(abbreviated FPdc)

YO, insert hook from **front** to **back** around post of st indicated ***(Fig. A)***, YO and pull up a loop (3 loops on hook), (YO and draw through 2 loops on hook) twice.

BACK POST DOUBLE CROCHET
(abbreviated BPdc)

YO, insert hook from **back** to **front** around post of st indicated ***(Fig. B)***, YO and pull up a loop (3 loops on hook), (YO and draw through 2 loops on hook) twice.

Fig. A

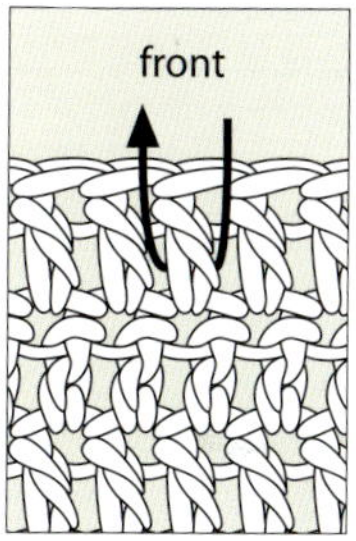

Fig. B

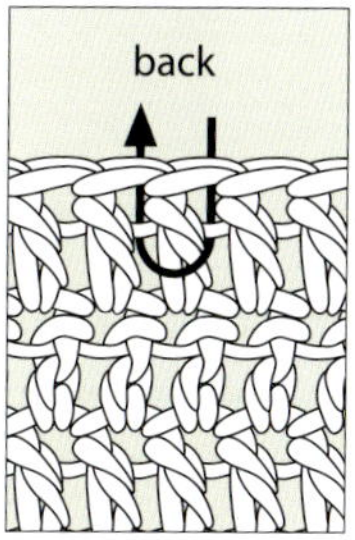

BOOT (Make 2)

SOLE (Make one in Tan and one in Green for each boot)

Ch 8{10}.

Rnd 1 (Right side)**:** Sc in second ch from hook and in each ch across to last ch, 4 hdc in last ch; working in free loops of beginning ch ***(Fig. 2, page 46)***, sc in next 5{7} chs, 3 sc in next ch; join with slip st to first sc: 18{22} sts.

Note: Loop a short piece of yarn around any stitch to mark Rnd 1 as **right** side.

Rnd 2: Ch 1, sc in same st as joining and in next 3{5} sc, hdc in next 2 sc, 2 dc in each of next 4 hdc, hdc in next 2 sc, sc in next 3{5} sc, 2 sc in each of last 3 sc; join with slip st to first sc: 25{29} sts.

Rnd 3: Ch 2 **(does not count as a st, now and throughout)**, hdc in same st as joining and in next 6{8} sts, 2 hdc in next dc, (hdc in next dc, 2 hdc in next dc) 3 times, hdc in next 5{7} sts, (sc in next sc, 2 sc in next sc) 3 times; join with slip st to first hdc, finish off: 32{36} sts.

On Green Sole, place split ring marker or scrap yarn in Front Loop Only of first hdc made on Rnd 3 for st placement ***(Fig. 3, page 46)***.

Joining: Hold two Soles with **wrong** sides together, matching sts, and Tan Sole facing you. Do **not** begin with slip knot on hook. Holding Green to the back and working through **both** loops of **both** pieces, insert hook in any st on Rnd 3, YO and pull up a loop, slip st in each st around; cut yarn. Remove hook from loop. Insert hook from **back** to **front** through center of first st, hook loop and draw through, YO and pull end through loop.

SIDES & TOE

Rnd 1 (Right side)**:** With Green Sole away from you and working in Back Loops Only, join Green with sc in marked loop ***(see Joining With Sc, page 46)***; remove marker, sc in each st around; join with slip st to first sc: 32{36} sc.

Rnd 2: Ch 1, working in both loops, sc in same st as joining and in next 11{13} sc, dc2tog 8 times, sc in last 4{6} sc; join with slip st to first sc: 24{28} sts.

Rnd 3: Ch 1, sc in same st as joining and in next 11{13} sc, dc2tog 4 times, sc in last 4{6} sc; join with slip st to first sc: 20{24} sts.

Rnd 4: Ch 1, sc in same st as joining and in next 11{13} sc, sc2tog twice, sc in last 4{6} sc; join with slip st to first sc, do **not** finish off: 18{22} sc.

CUFF

Size Small Only - Rnd 1: Ch 2, dc in same st as joining and in each sc around; join with slip st to first dc.

Size Medium Only - Rnd 1: Ch 2, dc in same st as joining and in each sc around to last 2 sc, dc2tog; join with slip st to first dc: 21 dc.

Both Sizes - Rnds 2-6: Ch 2, work FPdc around first st, work BPdc around each of next 2 sts, ★ work FPdc around next st, work BPdc around each of next 2 sts; repeat from ★ around; join with slip st to first FPdc.

Finish off.

Sew a button to Cuff having a right and left boot.

Casual Loafers

●●○○ EASY

SHOPPING LIST

Yarn (Medium Weight) MEDIUM 4

- ☐ Ecru - 40 yards (36.5 meters)
- ☐ Brown - 20 yards (18.5 meters)

Crochet Hook

- ☐ Size F (3.75 mm)
  or size needed for gauge

Additional Supplies

- ☐ Split ring marker or scrap yarn
- ☐ Yarn needle

SIZE INFORMATION

Small: 2" wide x 3" long (5 cm x 7.5 cm)
Medium: 2" wide x 3½" long (5 cm x 9 cm)

Size Note: We have printed the instructions for the sizes in different colors to make it easier for you to find:

- Size Small in Blue
- Size Medium in Pink

Instructions in Black apply to both sizes.

GAUGE INFORMATION

Gauge Swatch: 2" wide x 3{3½}" long [5 cm x 7.5{9} cm]
Work same as Sole.

STITCH GUIDE

SINGLE CROCHET 2 TOGETHER *(abbreviated sc2tog)*
Pull up a loop in each of next 2 sts, YO and draw through all 3 loops on hook **(counts as one sc)**.

LOAFER (Make 2)

SOLE (Make one in Ecru and one in Brown for each loafer)

Ch 8{10}.

Rnd 1 (Right side)**:** Sc in second ch from hook and in each ch across to last ch, 4 hdc in last ch; working in free loops of beginning ch ***(Fig. 2, page 46)***, sc in next 5{7} chs, 3 sc in next ch; join with slip st to first sc: 18{22} sts.

Note: Loop a short piece of yarn around any stitch to mark Rnd 1 as **right** side.

Rnd 2: Ch 1, sc in same st as joining and in next 3{5} sc, hdc in next 2 sc, 2 dc in each of next 4 hdc, hdc in next 2 sc, sc in next 3{5} sc, 2 sc in each of last 3 sc; join with slip st to first sc: 25{29} sts.

Rnd 3: Ch 2 **(does not count as a st)**, hdc in same st as joining and in next 6{8} sts, 2 hdc in next dc, (hdc in next dc, 2 hdc in next dc) 3 times, hdc in next 5{7} sts, (sc in next sc, 2 sc in next sc) 3 times; join with slip st to first hdc, finish off: 32{36} sts.

On Ecru Sole, place split ring marker or scrap yarn in Front Loop Only of first hdc made on Rnd 3 for st placement ***(Fig. 3, page 46)***.

Joining: Hold two Soles with **wrong** sides together, matching sts, and Brown Sole facing you. Do **not** begin with slip knot on hook. Holding Ecru to the back and working through **both** loops of **both** pieces, insert hook in any st on Rnd 3, YO and pull up a loop, slip st in each st around; cut yarn. Remove hook from loop. Insert hook from **back** to **front** through center of first st, hook loop and draw through, YO and pull end through loop.

SIDES & TOE

Rnd 1 (Right side)**:** With Ecru Sole away from you and working in Back Loops Only, join Ecru with sc in marked loop ***(see Joining With Sc, page 46)***; remove marker, sc in each st around; join with slip st to first sc: 32{36} sc.

Rnd 2: Ch 1, sc in both loops of each sc around; join with slip st to first sc.

Rnd 3: Ch 1, sc in same st as joining and in next 11{13} sc, working in Back Loops Only, sc2tog 8 times, sc in **both** loops of last 4{6} sc; join with slip st to first sc: 24{28} sc.

Rnd 4: Ch 1, sc in same st as joining and in next 11{13} sc, sc2tog 4 times, sc in last 4{6} sc; join with slip st to first sc: 20{24} sc.

Rnd 5: Ch 1, sc in same st as joining and in next 11{13} sc, sc2tog twice, sc in last 4{6} sc; join with slip st to first sc: 18{22} sc.

Rnd 6: Ch 1, sc in same st as joining and in next 12{14} sc, (slip st, ch 2, dc) in next sc, (dc, ch 2, slip st) in next sc, sc in last 3{5} sc; join with slip st to first sc; finish off.

Using photo as a guide for placement and a 12" (30.5 cm) length of Brown, weave through sts on last rnd.

HEEL TAB

With Brown, ch 4.

Row 1: Sc in second ch from hook and in each ch across: 3 sc.

Rows 2-10: Ch 1, turn; sc in each sc across.

Row 11: Turn; beginning in first sc, sc2tog, beginning in same st, sc2tog: 2 sc.

Row 12: Turn; beginning in first sc, sc2tog; finish off leaving a long end for sewing.

Placing beginning ch of Heel Tab to inside of loafer and last row on the outside, sew in place.

Motif Sandals

EASY

SHOPPING LIST

Yarn (Medium Weight) MEDIUM 4

- ☐ Pink - 30 yards (27.5 meters)
- ☐ Green - 30 yards (27.5 meters)

Crochet Hook

- ☐ Size F (3.75 mm)
  or size needed for gauge

Additional Supplies

- ☐ Split ring marker or scrap yarn
- ☐ Yarn needle

SIZE INFORMATION

Small: 2" wide x 3" long
(5 cm x 7.5 cm)
Medium: 2" wide x 3½" long
(5 cm x 9 cm)

Size Note: We have printed the instructions for the sizes in different colors to make it easier for you to find:
- Size Small in Blue
- Size Medium in Pink

Instructions in Black apply to both sizes.

GAUGE INFORMATION

Gauge Swatch: 2" wide x 3{3½}" long
[5 cm x 7.5{9} cm**]**
Work same as Sole.

SANDAL (Make 2)

SOLE (Make 2 for each sandal)

With Green, ch 8{10}.

Rnd 1 (Right side)**:** Sc in second ch from hook and in each ch across to last ch, 4 hdc in last ch; working in free loops of beginning ch ***(Fig. 2, page 46)***, sc in next 5{7} chs, 3 sc in next ch; join with slip st to first sc: 18{22} sts.

Note: Loop a short piece of yarn around any stitch to mark Rnd 1 as **right** side.

Rnd 2: Ch 1, sc in same st as joining and in next 3{5} sc, hdc in next 2 sc, 2 dc in each of next 4 hdc, hdc in next 2 sc, sc in next 3{5} sc, 2 sc in each of last 3 sc; join with slip st to first sc: 25{29} sts.

Rnd 3: Ch 2 (**does not count as a st, now and throughout**), hdc in same st as joining and in next 6{8} sts, 2 hdc in next dc, (hdc in next dc, 2 hdc in next dc) 3 times, hdc in next 5{7} sts, (sc in next sc, 2 sc in next sc) 3 times; join with slip st to first hdc, finish off: 32{36} sts.

On one Sole for each sandal, place split ring marker or scrap yarn in Front Loop Only of second{third} hdc made on Rnd 3 for st placement ***(Fig. 3, page 46)***.

Joining: Hold two Soles with **wrong** sides together, matching sts, and marked Sole on bottom. Do **not** begin with slip knot on hook. Holding Pink to the back and working through **both** loops of **both** pieces, insert hook in any st on Rnd 3, YO and pull up a loop, slip st in each st around; cut yarn. Remove hook from loop. Insert hook from **back** to **front** through center of first st, hook loop and draw through, YO and pull end through loop.

SIDES

Rnd 1 (Right side)**:** With marked Sole away from you and working in Back Loops Only, join Pink with dc in marked loop ***(see Joining With Dc, page 46)***; remove marker, dc in each st around; join with slip st to first dc: 32{36} dc.

Rnd 2: Ch 1, sc in both loops of each dc around; join with slip st to first sc, do **not** finish off.

HEEL

Row 1: Ch 1, sc in same st as joining and in next 9{11} sc, leave remaining 22{24} sc unworked: 10{12} sc.

Row 2: Ch 2, turn; dc in each sc across.

Row 3: Ch 1, turn; sc in each dc across; finish off.

MOTIF

Rnd 1 (Right side)**:** With Pink, ch 2; 9{10} sc in second ch from hook; join with slip st to first sc.

Note: Mark Rnd 1 as **right** side.

Rnd 2: Ch 3, dc around ch-3 ***(Fig. 4, page 47)***, (dc in next sc, dc around post of dc just made) around; join with slip st to top of beginning ch-3, finish off leaving a long end for sewing: 18{20} sts.

Skipping 5 sc on both sides of Heel, sew Motif to Sides across next 12{14} sts, leaving last 6 sts on Motif unworked.

TIE

With Green, ch 45; finish off.

Using photo as a guide for placement, fold chain in half and insert fold through a st on Rnd 2 of Motif from **right** side to **wrong** side; pull both ends through folded end. Weave each end through sc on Row 3 of Heel and tie in a bow at back.

Crossover Sandals

EASY

SHOPPING LIST

Yarn (Medium Weight) MEDIUM 4

- ☐ Tan - 30 yards (27.5 meters)
- ☐ Green - 30 yards (27.5 meters)

Crochet Hook

- ☐ Size F (3.75 mm)
  or size needed for gauge

Additional Supplies

- ☐ Split ring marker or scrap yarn
- ☐ 7/16" (11 mm) Button - 4
- ☐ Sewing needle and thread
- ☐ Yarn needle

SIZE INFORMATION

Small: 2" wide x 3" long
(5 cm x 7.5 cm)
Medium: 2" wide x 3½" long
(5 cm x 9 cm)

Size Note: We have printed the instructions for the sizes in different colors to make it easier for you to find:

- Size Small in Blue
- Size Medium in Pink

Instructions in Black apply to both sizes.

GAUGE INFORMATION

Gauge Swatch: 2" wide x 3{3½}" long
[5 cm x 7.5{9} cm]
Work same as Sole.

STITCH GUIDE

SINGLE CROCHET 2 TOGETHER
(abbreviated sc2tog)
Pull up a loop in each of next 2 sts, YO and draw through all 3 loops on hook **(counts as one sc)**.

SANDAL (Make 2)

SOLE (Make 2 for each sandal)

With Tan, ch 8{10}.

Rnd 1 (Right side)**:** Sc in second ch from hook and in each ch across to last ch, 4 hdc in last ch; working in free loops of beginning ch ***(Fig. 2, page 46)***, sc in next 5{7} chs, 3 sc in next ch; join with slip st to first sc: 18{22} sts.

Note: Loop a short piece of yarn around any stitch to mark Rnd 1 as **right** side.

Rnd 2: Ch 1, sc in same st as joining and in next 3{5} sc, hdc in next 2 sc, 2 dc in each of next 4 hdc, hdc in next 2 sc, sc in next 3{5} sc, 2 sc in each of last 3 sc; join with slip st to first sc: 25{29} sts.

Rnd 3: Ch 2 **(does not count as a st)**, hdc in same st as joining and in next 6{8} sts, 2 hdc in next dc, (hdc in next dc, 2 hdc in next dc) 3 times, hdc in next 5{7} sts, (sc in next sc, 2 sc in next sc) 3 times; join with slip st to first hdc, finish off: 32{36} sts.

On one Sole for each sandal, place split ring marker or scrap yarn in Front Loop Only of third hdc made on Rnd 3 for st placement ***(Fig. 3, page 46)***.

Joining: Hold two Soles with **wrong** sides together and matching sts. Using a double strand of Green, sew Soles together by weaving in and out of stitches on Rnd 3.

HEEL & STRAPS

Row 1 (Right side)**:** With Green, ch 8{10}; with marked Sole away from you and working in Back Loops Only, sc in marked loop; remove marker, sc in next 11 sts, ch 9{11}, leave remaining 20{24} sts unworked: 29{33} sts.

Row 2: Turn; working in back ridge of chs ***(Fig. 1, page 46)***, 2 sc in second ch from hook, sc in next 7{9} chs, dc in **both** loops of next 12 sc, working in back ridge of chs, sc in next 7{9} chs, 2 sc in last ch: 30{34} sts.

Row 3: Ch 1, turn; sc in first sc, ch 1, skip next sc **(buttonhole)**, sc in each st across to last 2 sc, ch 1, skip next sc **(buttonhole)**, sc in last sc: 28{32} sc and 2 chs.

Row 4: Turn; beginning in first sc, sc2tog, sc in each sc across to last ch, sc2tog: 28{32} sc.

Row 5: Turn; slip st in each sc across; finish off.

TOE STRAP

With Green, ch 9.

Row 1 (Right side)**:** Sc in back ridge of second ch from hook and each ch across: 8 sc.

Note: Mark Row 1 as **right** side.

Rows 2 and 3: Ch 1, turn; sc in each sc across.

Finish off leaving a long end for sewing.

Skip 5 sts from Heel and sew end of rows on Toe Strap to Sole. Repeat with opposite end.

Sew 2 buttons to Toe Strap, 2 sc from each edge. Cross Heel Straps and button in place.

Espadrilles

EASY

SHOPPING LIST

Yarn (Medium Weight) MEDIUM 4

- ☐ Coral - 30 yards (27.5 meters)
- ☐ Off White - 30 yards (27.5 meters)

Crochet Hook

- ☐ Size F (3.75 mm)

  or size needed for gauge

Additional Supplies

- ☐ Split ring marker or scrap yarn
- ☐ Yarn needle

SIZE INFORMATION

Small: 2" wide x 3" long (5 cm x 7.5 cm)

Medium: 2" wide x 3½" long (5 cm x 9 cm)

Size Note: We have printed the instructions for the sizes in different colors to make it easier for you to find:

- Size Small in Blue
- Size Medium in Pink

Instructions in Black apply to both sizes.

GAUGE INFORMATION

Gauge Swatch: 2" wide x 3{3½}" long [5 cm x 7.5{9} cm]

Work same as Sole.

STITCH GUIDE

CLUSTER (uses one sc)

★ YO, insert hook in sc indicated, YO and pull up a loop, YO and draw through 2 loops on hook; repeat from ★ 2 times **more**, YO and draw through all 4 loops on hook.

SINGLE CROCHET 2 TOGETHER ***(abbreviated sc2tog)***

Pull up a loop in each of next 2 sts, YO and draw through all 3 loops on hook **(counts as one sc)**.

SINGLE CROCHET 3 TOGETHER ***(abbreviated sc3tog)***

Pull up a loop in each of next 3 sts, YO and draw through all 4 loops on hook **(counts as one sc)**.

ESPADRILLE (Make 2)

SOLE (Make 2 for each Espadrille)

With Off White, ch 8{10}.

Rnd 1 (Right side)**:** Sc in second ch from hook and in each ch across to last ch, 4 hdc in last ch; working in free loops of beginning ch ***(Fig. 2, page 46)***, sc in next 5{7} chs, 3 sc in next ch; join with slip st to first sc: 18{22} sts.

Note: Loop a short piece of yarn around any stitch to mark Rnd 1 as **right** side.

Rnd 2: Ch 1, sc in same st as joining and in next 3{5} sc, hdc in next 2 sc, 2 dc in each of next 4 hdc, hdc in next 2 sc, sc in next 3{5} sc, 2 sc in each of last 3 sc; join with slip st to first sc: 25{29} sts.

Rnd 3: Ch 2 (**does not count as a st, now and throughout**), hdc in same st as joining and in next 6{8} sts, 2 hdc in next dc, (hdc in next dc, 2 hdc in next dc) 3 times, hdc in next 5{7} sts, (sc in next sc, 2 sc in next sc) 3 times; join with slip st to first hdc, finish off: 32{36} sts.

On one Sole for each espadrille, place split ring marker or scrap yarn in Front Loop Only of third{fifth} hdc made on Rnd 3 for st placement ***(Fig. 3, page 46)***.

Joining: Hold two Soles with **wrong** sides together, matching sts, and marked Sole on bottom. Do **not** begin with slip knot on hook. Holding Coral to the back and working through **both** loops of **both** pieces, insert hook in any st on Rnd 3, YO and pull up a loop, slip st in each st around; cut yarn. Remove hook from loop. Insert hook from **back** to **front** through center of first st, hook loop and draw through, YO and pull end through loop.

HEEL

Row 1 (Right side)**:** With marked Sole away from you and working in Back Loops Only, join Coral with sc in marked loop ***(see Joining With Sc, page 46)***; remove marker, sc in next 13{17} sts, leave remaining 18 sts unworked: 14{18} sc.

Row 2: Ch 2, turn; dc in both loops of each sc across.

Row 3: Ch 1, turn; sc in each dc across; finish off.

TOE

Row 1 (Right side)**:** With **right** side of Heel facing and working in Back Loops Only on Sole, join Coral with sc in same st as last sc on Heel; sc in next 18 sts, sc in same st as first sc on Heel: 20 sc.

Row 2: Ch 1, turn; working in both loops, sc in first sc, (ch 1, skip next sc, hdc in next sc) 9 times, sc in last sc: 11 sts and 9 ch-1 sps.

Row 3: Ch 1, turn; sc in first 2 sts and in each ch-1 sp across, sc in last sc: 12 sc.

Row 4: Ch 1, turn; sc in first sc, (skip next sc, work Cluster in next sc) across to last sc, sc in last sc: 2 sc and 5 Clusters.

Row 5: Turn; beginning in first sc, sc2tog, sc3tog, sc2tog; finish off.

EDGING

Row 1: With **right** side facing and working in end of rows, join Coral with slip st in Row 1; work 10 slip sts evenly spaced across top edge of Toe: 11 sts.

Row 2: Turn; working in Front Loops Only, slip st in first st, (ch 2, skip next st, slip st in next st) across; finish off.

Sew end of rows on Heel behind Toe Edging.

Flower Petal Slippers

●●○○ EASY

SHOPPING LIST

Yarn (Medium Weight) MEDIUM 4

- ☐ Yellow - 30 yards (27.5 meters)
- ☐ White - 20 yards (18.5 meters)
- ☐ Aqua - 10 yards (9 meters)

Crochet Hook

- ☐ Size F (3.75 mm)
  or size needed for gauge

Additional Supplies

- ☐ Split ring marker or scrap yarn
- ☐ ½" (12 mm) Button - 2
- ☐ Sewing needle and thread

SIZE INFORMATION

Small: 2" wide x 3" long
(5 cm x 7.5 cm)

Medium: 2" wide x 3½" long
(5 cm x 9 cm)

Size Note: We have printed the instructions for the sizes in different colors to make it easier for you to find:

- Size Small in Blue
- Size Medium in Pink

Instructions in Black apply to both sizes.

GAUGE INFORMATION

Gauge Swatch: 2" wide x 3{3½}" long
[5 cm x 7.5{9} cm]

Work same as Sole.

STITCH GUIDE

SINGLE CROCHET 2 TOGETHER
(abbreviated sc2tog)

Pull up a loop in each of next 2 sts, YO and draw through all 3 loops on hook **(counts as one sc)**.

SLIPPER (Make 2)

SOLE (Make 2 for each slipper)

With Yellow, ch 8{10}.

Rnd 1 (Right side)**:** Sc in second ch from hook and in each ch across to last ch, 4 hdc in last ch; working in free loops of beginning ch *(Fig. 2, page 46)*, sc in next 5{7} chs, 3 sc in next ch; join with slip st to first sc: 18{22} sts.

Note: Loop a short piece of yarn around any stitch to mark Rnd 1 as **right** side.

Rnd 2: Ch 1, sc in same st as joining and in next 3{5} sc, hdc in next 2 sc, 2 dc in each of next 4 hdc, hdc in next 2 sc, sc in next 3{5} sc, 2 sc in each of last 3 sc; join with slip st to first sc: 25{29} sts.

Rnd 3: Ch 2 **(does not count as a st)**, hdc in same st as joining and in next 6{8} sts, 2 hdc in next dc, (hdc in next dc, 2 hdc in next dc) 3 times, hdc in next 5{7} sts, (sc in next sc, 2 sc in next sc) 3 times; join with slip st to first hdc, finish off: 32{36} sts.

On one Sole for each slipper, place split ring marker or scrap yarn in Front Loop Only of second{third} hdc made on Rnd 3 for st placement *(Fig. 3, page 46)*.

Joining: Hold two Soles with **wrong** sides together, matching sts, and marked Sole on bottom. Do **not** begin with slip knot on hook. Holding Aqua to the back and working through **both** loops of **both** pieces, insert hook in any st on Rnd 3, YO and pull up a loop, slip st in each st around; cut yarn. Remove hook from loop. Insert hook from **back** to **front** through center of first st, hook loop and draw through, YO and pull end through loop.

SIDES & TOE

Rnd 1 (Right side)**:** With marked Sole away from you and working in Back Loops Only, join White with sc in marked loop *(see Joining With Sc, page 46)*; remove marker, sc in each st around; join with slip st to first sc: 32{36} sc.

Rnd 2: Ch 1, sc in both loops of each sc around; join with slip st to first sc.

Rnd 3: Ch 1, sc in same st as joining and in next 12{15} sc, sc2tog 8 times, sc in last 3{4} sc; join with slip st to first sc: 24{28} sc.

Rnd 4: Ch 1, sc in same st as joining and in next 12{15} sc, sc2tog 4 times, sc in last 3{4} sc; join with slip st to first sc, do **not** finish off: 20{24} sts.

HEEL

Row 1: Ch 1, sc in same st as joining and in next 9{11} sc, leave remaining 10{12} sc unworked.

Row 2: Ch 1, turn; sc in each sc across; finish off.

TRIM

TOE TRIM

Do **not** begin with slip knot on hook. With **right** side facing and using Aqua, insert hook in first unworked st on Rnd 4 of Toe, YO and pull up a loop, slip st in each st across; cut yarn. Insert hook from **back** to **front** through center of next st, hook loop and draw through, YO and pull end through loop.

RIGHT SLIPPER

With **wrong** side facing, join Aqua with slip st in end of first sc on Row 2 of Heel; ch 11{13}, slip st in fifth ch from hook **(buttonhole made)**, working in chs and in Back Loops Only of sc on Heel, ★ skip next st, 5 dc in next st, skip next st, slip st in next st; repeat from ★ across; finish off.

LEFT SLIPPER

With **wrong** side facing, join Aqua with slip st in end of last sc on Row 2 of Heel; ch 11{13}, slip st in fifth ch from hook **(buttonhole made)**, finish off.

With **wrong** side facing and working in Back Loops Only on Row 2 of Heel, join Aqua with slip st in first sc; working in sc and in chs, ★ skip next st, 5 dc in next st, skip next st, slip st in next st; repeat from ★ across ending in same ch as slip st for buttonhole; finish off.

Sew button to Heel opposite strap.

High-Top Moccasins

●●○○ **EASY**

SHOPPING LIST

Yarn (Medium Weight)

- ☐ Ecru - 85 yards (77.5 meters)
- ☐ Brown - 15 yards (13.5 meters)
- ☐ Aqua - small amount
- ☐ Red - small amount

Crochet Hook

- ☐ Size F (3.75 mm)
  or size needed for gauge

Additional Supplies

- ☐ Split ring marker or scrap yarn
- ☐ Yarn needle

SIZE INFORMATION

Small: 2" wide x 3" long
(5 cm x 7.5 cm)
Medium: 2" wide x 3½" long
(5 cm x 9 cm)

Size Note: We have printed the instructions for the sizes in different colors to make it easier for you to find:

- Size Small in Blue
- Size Medium in Pink

Instructions in Black apply to both sizes.

GAUGE INFORMATION

Gauge Swatch: 2" wide x 3{3½}" long
[5 cm x 7.5{9} cm]
Work same as Sole.

STITCH GUIDE

SPLIT SINGLE CROCHET
(abbreviated Split sc)
Insert hook between legs of next st ***(Fig. A)***, YO and pull up a loop, YO and draw through both loops on hook.

Fig. A

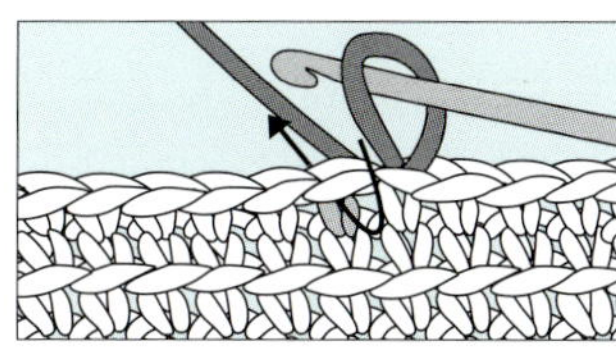

DOUBLE CROCHET 2 TOGETHER
(abbreviated dc2tog) (uses next 2 sts)
★ YO, insert hook in **next** st, YO and pull up a loop, YO and draw through 2 loops on hook; repeat from ★ once **more**, YO and draw through all 3 loops on hook **(counts as one dc)**.

MOCCASIN (Make 2)

SOLE

(Make one in Ecru and one in Brown for each moccasin)

Ch 8{10}.

Rnd 1 (Right side)**:** Sc in second ch from hook and in each ch across to last ch, 4 hdc in last ch; working in free loops of beginning ch (***Fig. 2, page 46***), sc in next 5{7} chs, 3 sc in next ch; join with slip st to first sc: 18{22} sts.

Note: Loop a short piece of yarn around any stitch to mark Rnd 1 as **right** side.

Rnd 2: Ch 1, sc in same st as joining and in next 3{5} sc, hdc in next 2 sc, 2 dc in each of next 4 hdc, hdc in next 2 sc, sc in next 3{5} sc, 2 sc in each of last 3 sc; join with slip st to first sc: 25{29} sts.

Rnd 3: Ch 2 **(does not count as a st)**, hdc in same st as joining and in next 6{8} sts, 2 hdc in next dc, (hdc in next dc, 2 hdc in next dc) 3 times, hdc in next 5{7} sts, (sc in next sc, 2 sc in next sc) 3 times; join with slip st to first hdc, finish off: 32{36} sts.

On Ecru Sole, place split ring marker or scrap yarn in Front Loop Only of first hdc made on Rnd 3 for st placement ***(Fig. 3, page 46)***.

Joining: Hold two Soles with **wrong** sides together, matching sts, and Brown Sole facing you. Do **not** begin with slip knot on hook. Holding Ecru to the back and working through **both** loops of **both** pieces, insert hook in any st on Rnd 3, YO and pull up a loop, slip st in each st around; cut yarn. Remove hook from loop. Insert hook from **back** to **front** through center of first st, hook loop and draw through, YO and pull end through loop.

SIDES & TOE

Rnd 1 (Right side)**:** With Ecru Sole away from you and working in Back Loops Only, join Ecru with sc in marked loop ***(see Joining With Sc, page 46)***; remove marker, sc in each st around; join with slip st to first sc: 32{36} sc.

Rnd 2: Ch 1, sc in both loops of each sc around; join with slip st to first sc.

Rnd 3: Ch 1, sc in same st as joining and in next 11{13} sc, working in Back Loops Only, dc2tog 8 times, sc in **both** loops of last 4{6} sc; join with slip st to first sc: 24{28} sts.

Rnd 4: Ch 1, sc in same st as joining and in next 11{13} sc, dc2tog 4 times, sc in last 4{6} sc; join with slip st to first sc: 20{24} sts.

Rnd 5: Ch 1, sc in same st as joining and in next 11{13} sc, dc2tog twice, sc in last 4{6} sc; join with slip st to first sc: 18{22} sc.

Rnds 6-11: Ch 1, sc in each sc around; join with slip st to first sc.

Rnd 12: Ch 1, sc in Back Loop Only of each sc around; join with slip st to first sc.

Rnd 13: Ch 1, work Split sc in each sc around; join with slip st to first Split sc.

Rnd 14: Ch 1, work Split sc in each Split sc around; join with slip st to first Split sc.

Rnd 15: Ch 1, sc in Back Loop Only of each st around; join with slip st to first sc, finish off.

DUPLICATE SPLIT SC

Duplicate Split sc is worked over the first Split sc rnd (Rnd 13). Each stitch forms a V and you want to completely cover that V so that the design appears to have been worked into the fabric. Thread a yarn needle with an 18" (45.5 cm) length of Aqua.

With **right** side facing and beginning at first stitch on Rnd 13, bring the needle up from the **wrong** side between the strands of yarn on Rnd 12 at the base of the V, leaving an end to be woven in later ***(Fig. B)***. Follow the right side of the V up and insert the needle from **right** to **left** under the strands of the V immediately above, keeping the yarn on top of the stitch ***(Fig. C)***, and draw through. Insert the needle back through the bottom of the same stitch where the first stitch began ***(Duplicate Split sc completed)***.

Work over every other stitch around, matching tension of fabric to avoid puckering.

Fig. B

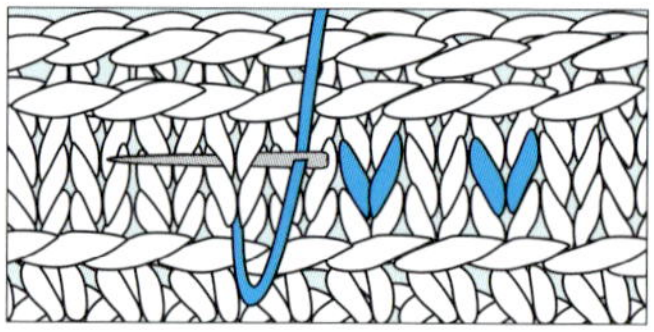

Fig. C

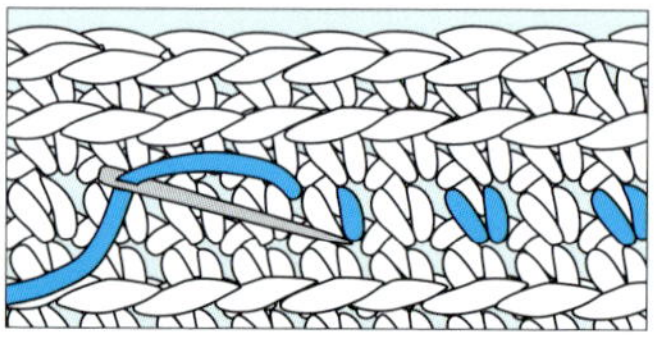

With Red, work duplicate Split sc over each unworked stitch on Rnd 13.

FRINGE

Cut a piece of cardboard 2" (5 cm) square. Wind the yarn **loosely** and **evenly** around the cardboard until the card is filled, then cut across one end; repeat as needed.

Fold one strand of yarn in half.

Insert hook from top to bottom in free loop of first stitch on Rnd 11 (unused loop after working in back loops). Draw the folded end up through the stitch and pull the loose ends through the folded end ***(Fig. D)***; draw the knot up tightly ***(Fig. E)***. Repeat in each stitch around. Trim the ends.

Fig. D

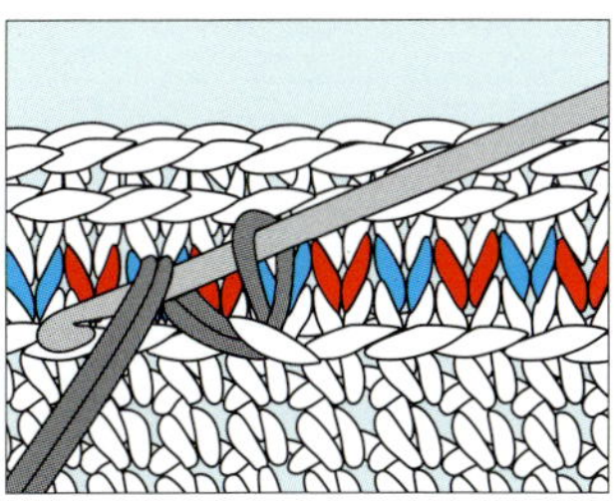

Fig. E

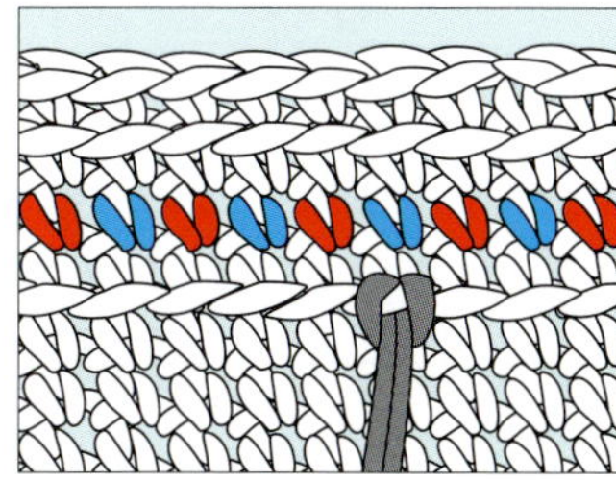

TRIM

Using photo as a guide for placement and beginning at opposite sides of boots for right and left boot, weave Red through stitches on last rnd; tie in a bow.

High-Top Sneakers

EASY

SHOPPING LIST

Yarn (Medium Weight) MEDIUM 4

- ☐ White - 52 yards (47.5 meters)
- ☐ Blue - 52 yards (47.5 meters)
- ☐ Red - small amount

Crochet Hook

- ☐ Size F (3.75 mm)
  or size needed for gauge

Additional Supplies

- ☐ Split ring marker or scrap yarn
- ☐ Yarn needle

SIZE INFORMATION

Small: 2" wide x 3" long
(5 cm x 7.5 cm)

Medium: 2" wide x 3½" long
(5 cm x 9 cm)

Size Note: We have printed the instructions for the sizes in different colors to make it easier for you to find:

- Size Small in Blue
- Size Medium in Pink

Instructions in Black apply to both sizes.

GAUGE INFORMATION

Gauge Swatch: 2" wide x 3{3½}" long
[5 cm x 7.5{9} cm**]**

Work same as Sole.

STITCH GUIDE

SINGLE CROCHET 2 TOGETHER
(abbreviated sc2tog)

Pull up a loop in each of next 2 sts, YO and draw through all 3 loops on hook **(counts as one sc)**.

DOUBLE CROCHET 2 TOGETHER
(abbreviated dc2tog)
(uses next 2 sts)

★ YO, insert hook in **next** st, YO and pull up a loop, YO and draw through 2 loops on hook; repeat from ★ once **more**, YO and draw through all 3 loops on hook **(counts as one dc)**.

SNEAKER (Make 2)

SOLE (Make 2 for each sneaker)

With White, ch 8{10}.

Rnd 1 (Right side)**:** Sc in second ch from hook and in each ch across to last ch, 4 hdc in last ch; working in free loops of beginning ch *(Fig. 2, page 46)*, sc in next 5{7} chs, 3 sc in next ch; join with slip st to first sc: 18{22} sts.

Note: Loop a short piece of yarn around any stitch to mark Rnd 1 as **right** side.

Rnd 2: Ch 1, sc in same st as joining and in next 3{5} sc, hdc in next 2 sc, 2 dc in each of next 4 hdc, hdc in next 2 sc, sc in next 3{5} sc, 2 sc in each of last 3 sc; join with slip st to first sc: 25{29} sts.

Rnd 3: Ch 2 (**does not count as a st, now and throughout**), hdc in same st as joining and in next 6{8} sts, 2 hdc in next dc, (hdc in next dc, 2 hdc in next dc) 3 times, hdc in next 5{7} sts, (sc in next sc, 2 sc in next sc) 3 times; join with slip st to first hdc, finish off: 32{36} sts.

On one Sole, place split ring marker or scrap yarn in Front Loop Only of fifth{seventh} hdc made on Rnd 3 for st placement *(Fig. 3, page 46)*.

Joining: Hold two Soles with **wrong** sides together, matching sts, and marked Sole on bottom. Do **not** begin with slip knot on hook. Holding Red to the back and working through **both** loops of **both** pieces, insert hook in any st on Rnd 3, YO and pull up a loop, slip st in each st around; cut yarn. Remove hook from loop. Insert hook from **back** to **front** through center of first st, hook loop and draw through, YO and pull end through loop.

SIDES

Row 1 (Right side)**:** With marked Sole away from you and working in Back Loops Only, join Blue with sc in marked loop *(see Joining With Sc, page 46)*; remove marker, sc in next 15{19} sts, leave remaining 16 sts unworked: 16{20} sc.

Row 2: Ch 2, turn; dc in both loops of each sc across.

Row 3: Ch 1, turn; sc in each dc across.

Rows 4 thru 6{8}: Repeat Rows 2 and 3, 1{2} time(s); then repeat Row 2 once **more**.

Finish off.

Trim: With **right** side facing, join Red with slip st in first dc on Sides; slip st in each dc across; finish off.

TOE

Row 1: With **right** side facing and working in Back Loops Only of Sole, join White with sc in first unworked st; sc in each sc across: 16 sc.

Row 2: Ch 1, turn; working in both loops, sc in first sc, hdc in next 3 sc, dc in next 8 sc, hdc in next 3 sc, sc in last sc.

Row 3: Turn; working in Back Loops Only and beginning in first sc, sc2tog twice, dc2tog 4 times, sc2tog twice: 8 sts.

Row 4: Ch 1, turn; working in both loops, sc in first 2 sc, dc in next 4 dc, sc in last 2 sc; finish off.

TONGUE

Row 1: With **right** side facing, join Blue with sc in first sc on Toe; sc in each st across.

Rows 2 thru 9{11}: Ch 1, turn; sc in each sc across.

Finish off.

With White, sew end of first 3 rows on Sides to end of rows on Toe.

LACES

With White, ch 80{85}; finish off.

Using photo as a guide for placement and beginning at the bottom of the Sides, weave Laces through end of rows.

Lacy Cuff Boots

●●○○○ EASY

SHOPPING LIST

Yarn (Medium Weight) MEDIUM 4

- ☐ Grey - 80 yards (73 meters)
- ☐ Lavender - 30 yards (27.5 meters)
- ☐ White - small amount
- ☐ Pink - small amount

Crochet Hook

- ☐ Size F (3.75 mm) **or** size needed for gauge

Additional Supplies

- ☐ Split ring marker or scrap yarn
- ☐ Yarn needle

SIZE INFORMATION

Small: 2" wide x 3" long
(5 cm x 7.5 cm)
Medium: 2" wide x 3½" long
(5 cm x 9 cm)

Size Note: We have printed the instructions for the sizes in different colors to make it easier for you to find:

- Size Small in Blue
- Size Medium in Pink

Instructions in Black apply to both sizes.

GAUGE INFORMATION

Gauge Swatch: 2" wide x 3{3½}" long
[5 cm x 7.5{9} cm]
Work same as Sole.

STITCH GUIDE

TREBLE CROCHET ***(abbreviated tr)***
YO twice, insert hook in st indicated, YO and pull up a loop (4 loops on hook), (YO and draw through 2 loops on hook) 3 times.

SINGLE CROCHET 2 TOGETHER ***(abbreviated sc2tog)***
Pull up a loop in each of next 2 sts, YO and draw through all 3 loops on hook **(counts as one sc)**.

DOUBLE CROCHET 2 TOGETHER ***(abbreviated dc2tog)***
(uses next 2 sts)
★ YO, insert hook in **next** st, YO and pull up a loop, YO and draw through 2 loops on hook; repeat from ★ once **more**, YO and draw through all 3 loops on hook **(counts as one dc)**.

BOOT (Make 2)

SOLE (Make 2 for each boot)

With Grey, ch 8{10}.

Rnd 1 (Right side)**:** Sc in second ch from hook and in each ch across to last ch, 4 hdc in last ch; working in free loops of beginning ch ***(Fig. 2, page 46)***, sc in next 5{7} chs, 3 sc in next ch; join with slip st to first sc: 18{22} sts.

Note: Loop a short piece of yarn around any stitch to mark Rnd 1 as **right** side.

Rnd 2: Ch 1, sc in same st as joining and in next 3{5} sc, hdc in next 2 sc, 2 dc in each of next 4 hdc, hdc in next 2 sc, sc in next 3{5} sc, 2 sc in each of last 3 sc; join with slip st to first sc: 25{29} sts.

Rnd 3: Ch 2 (**does not count as a st**), hdc in same st as joining and in next 6{8} sts, 2 hdc in next dc, (hdc in next dc, 2 hdc in next dc) 3 times, hdc in next 5{7} sts, (sc in next sc, 2 sc in next sc) 3 times; join with slip st to first hdc, finish off: 32{36} sts.

On one Sole for each boot, place split ring marker or scrap yarn in Front Loop Only of first hdc made on Rnd 3 for st placement ***(Fig. 3, page 46)***.

Joining: Hold two Soles with **wrong** sides together, matching sts, and marked Sole on bottom. Do **not** begin with slip knot on hook. Holding Lavender to the back and working through **both** loops of **both** pieces, insert hook in any st on Rnd 3, YO and pull up a loop, slip st in each st around; cut yarn. Remove hook from loop. Insert hook from **back** to **front** through center of first st, hook loop and draw through, YO and pull end through loop.

SIDES & TOE

Rnd 1 (Right side)**:** With marked Sole away from you and working in Back Loops Only, join Grey with sc in marked loop ***(see Joining With Sc, page 46)***; remove marker, sc in each st around; drop Grey, with Lavender, join with slip st to first sc ***(Fig. 6, page 47)***: 32{36} sc.

Rnd 2: Ch 1, sc in both loops of each sc around; drop Lavender, with Grey, join with slip st to first sc.

Rnd 3: Ch 1, sc in same st as joining and in next 11{13} sc, dc2tog 8 times, sc in next 4{6} sc; drop Grey, with Lavender, join with slip st to first sc: 24{28} sts.

Rnd 4: Ch 1, sc in same st as joining and in next 11{13} sc, dc2tog 4 times, sc in next 4{6} sc; drop Lavender, with Grey, join with slip st to first sc: 20{24} sts.

Rnd 5: Ch 1, sc in same st as joining and in next 11{13} sc, dc2tog twice, sc in last 4{6} sc; drop Grey, with Lavender, join with slip st to first sc: 18{22} sc.

Rnd 6: Ch 1, sc in same st as joining and in next 11{13} sc, sc2tog, sc in last 4{6} sc; cut Lavender, with Grey, join with slip st to first sc: 17{21} sc.

Rnd 7: Ch 1, sc in each sc around; do **not** join, place marker to indicate beginning of rnd ***(see Markers, page 45)***.

Rnds 8-13: Sc in each sc around.

Slip st in next sc, finish off.

LACY CUFF

Size Small Only - Rnd 1: With **wrong** side facing and working in Back Loops Only, join Lavender with sc in same st as slip st; (sc in next 3 sc, 2 sc in next sc) around; join with slip st to first sc: 21 sc.

Size Medium Only - Rnd 1: With **wrong** side facing and working in Back Loops Only, join Lavender with sc in same st as slip st; sc in next 5 sc, 2 sc in next sc, (sc in next 6 sc, 2 sc in next sc) twice; join with slip st to first sc: 24 sc.

Both Sizes - Rnd 2: Ch 4 **(counts as first tr)**, turn; skip next 4 sc, tr in next sc, ch 1, working in **front** of tr just made ***(Fig. 5a, page 47)***, tr in third skipped sc, ★ skip next 2 sc, tr in next sc, ch 1, working in **front** of tr just made, tr in first skipped sc; repeat from ★ around, working **behind** first tr ***(Fig. 5b, page 47)***, tr in second skipped sc, ch 1; join with slip st to first tr: 14{16} tr and 7{8} ch-1 sps.

Rnd 3: Ch 1, turn; sc in same st as joining and in each ch-1 sp and each tr around; join with slip st to first sc: 21{24} sc.

Rnd 4: Repeat Rnd 2.

Rnd 5: Ch 3, turn; slip st in same st as joining, (slip st, ch 3, slip st) in each ch-1 sp and in each tr around; finish off.

Fold Cuff down.

FLOWER

With Pink, ch 4; join with slip st to form a ring.

Rnd 1 (Right side)**:** 6 Sc in ring; join with slip st to first sc, finish off leaving a long end for sewing.

Note: Mark Rnd 1 as **right** side.

Rnd 2: With **right** side facing, join White with slip st in first sc, ch 2, (dc, ch 1, slip st) in same st, (slip st, ch 2, dc, ch 1, slip st) in each sc around; join with slip st to joining slip st, finish off.

Using photo as a guide for placement, sew a Flower to each Cuff having a right and left boot.

Peek-a-Boo Sandals

EASY

SHOPPING LIST

Yarn (Medium Weight) 4 MEDIUM

- ☐ Orchid - 35 yards (32 meters)
- ☐ Grey - 20 yards (18.5 meters)
- ☐ Gold - small amount

Crochet Hook

- ☐ Size F (3.75 mm)
  or size needed for gauge

Additional Supplies

- ☐ Split ring marker or scrap yarn
- ☐ Yarn needle

SIZE INFORMATION

Small: 2" wide x 3" long
(5 cm x 7.5 cm)
Medium: 2" wide x 3½" long
(5 cm x 9 cm)

Size Note: We have printed the instructions for the sizes in different colors to make it easier for you to find:

- Size Small in Blue
- Size Medium in Pink

Instructions in Black apply to both sizes.

GAUGE INFORMATION

Gauge Swatch: 2" wide x 3{3½}" long
[5 cm x 7.5{9} cm]
Work same as Sole.

SANDAL (Make 2)

SOLE (Make 2 for each sandal)

With Orchid, ch 8{10}.

Rnd 1 (Right side)**:** Sc in second ch from hook and in each ch across to last ch, 4 hdc in last ch; working in free loops of beginning ch ***(Fig. 2, page 46)***, sc in next 5{7} chs, 3 sc in next ch; join with slip st to first sc: 18{22} sts.

Note: Loop a short piece of yarn around any stitch to mark Rnd 1 as **right** side.

Rnd 2: Ch 1, sc in same st as joining and in next 3{5} sc, hdc in next 2 sc, 2 dc in each of next 4 hdc, hdc in next 2 sc, sc in next 3{5} sc, 2 sc in each of last 3 sc; join with slip st to first sc: 25{29} sts.

Rnd 3: Ch 2 **(does not count as a st)**, hdc in same st as joining and in next 6{8} sts, 2 hdc in next dc, (hdc in next dc, 2 hdc in next dc) 3 times, hdc in next 5{7} sts, (sc in next sc, 2 sc in next sc) 3 times; join with slip st to first hdc, finish off: 32{36} sts.

On one Sole for each sandal, place split ring marker or scrap yarn in Front Loop Only of ninth{eleventh} hdc made on Rnd 3 for st placement ***(Fig. 3, page 46)***.

Joining: Hold two Soles with **wrong** sides together, matching sts, and marked Sole facing you. Do **not** begin with slip knot on hook. Holding Gold to the back and working through **both** loops of **both** pieces, insert hook in any st on Rnd 3, YO and pull up a loop, slip st in each st around; cut yarn. Remove hook from loop. Insert hook from **back** to **front** through center of first st, hook loop and draw through, YO and pull end through loop.

SIDES

Row 1 (Right side)**:** With marked Sole away from you and working in Back Loops Only, join Grey with sc in marked loop ***(see Joining With Sc, page 46)***; remove marker, sc in next 24{28} sts, leave remaining 7 hdc unworked: 25{29} sts.

Rows 2-5: Ch 1, turn; sc in both loops of each sc across.

Finish off leaving a long end for sewing.

Sew top 2 corners together.

FLOWER

CENTER (Right side)

With Gold, ch 2; 4 sc in second ch from hook; join with slip st to first sc, finish off leaving a long end for sewing.

PETALS

Rnd 1 (Right side)**:** With Orchid, ch 2; 5 sc in second ch from hook; do **not** join.

Rnd 2: (Slip st, ch 3, 2 dc, ch 2, slip st) in each sc around; finish off leaving a long end for sewing.

Sew Center to Petals. Using photo as a guide for placement, sew Flower to joined corners of Sides.

Sporty Sneakers

EASY

SHOPPING LIST

Yarn (Medium Weight) 4

- ☐ Tan - 30 yards (27.5 meters)
- ☐ Blue - 25 yards (23 meters)
- ☐ Off White - small amount

Crochet Hook

- ☐ Size F (3.75 mm)

  or size needed for gauge

Additional Supplies

- ☐ Split ring marker or scrap yarn
- ☐ Yarn needle

SIZE INFORMATION

Small: 2" wide x 3" long (5 cm x 7.5 cm)
Medium: 2" wide x 3½" long (5 cm x 9 cm)

Size Note: We have printed the instructions for the sizes in different colors to make it easier for you to find:

· Size Small in Blue
· Size Medium in Pink

Instructions in Black apply to both sizes.

GAUGE INFORMATION

Gauge Swatch: 2" wide x 3{3½}" long
[5 cm x 7.5{9} cm]

Work same as Sole.

STITCH GUIDE

SINGLE CROCHET 2 TOGETHER ***(abbreviated sc2tog)***

Pull up a loop in each of next 2 sts, YO and draw through all 3 loops on hook **(counts as one sc)**.

DOUBLE CROCHET 2 TOGETHER ***(abbreviated dc2tog)***
(uses next 2 sts)

★ YO, insert hook in **next** st, YO and pull up a loop, YO and draw through 2 loops on hook; repeat from ★ once **more**, YO and draw through all 3 loops on hook **(counts as one dc)**.

SNEAKER (Make 2)

SOLE (Make 2 for each sneaker)

With Tan, ch 8{10}.

Rnd 1 (Right side)**:** Sc in second ch from hook and in each ch across to last ch, 4 hdc in last ch; working in free loops of beginning ch ***(Fig. 2, page 46)***, sc in next 5{7} chs, 3 sc in next ch; join with slip st to first sc: 18{22} sts.

Note: Loop a short piece of yarn around any stitch to mark Rnd 1 as **right** side.

Rnd 2: Ch 1, sc in same st as joining and in next 3{5} sc, hdc in next 2 sc, 2 dc in each of next 4 hdc, hdc in next 2 sc, sc in next 3{5} sc, 2 sc in each of last 3 sc; join with slip st to first sc: 25{29} sts.

Rnd 3: Ch 2 **(does not count as a st)**, hdc in same st as joining and in next 6{8} sts, 2 hdc in next dc, (hdc in next dc, 2 hdc in next dc) 3 times, hdc in next 5{7} sts, (sc in next sc, 2 sc in next sc) 3 times; join with slip st to first hdc, finish off: 32{36} sts.

On one Sole for each sneaker, place split ring marker or scrap yarn in Front Loop Only of third hdc made on Rnd 3 for st placement ***(Fig. 3, page 46)***.

Joining: Hold two Soles with **wrong** sides together, matching sts, and marked Sole on bottom. Do **not** begin with slip knot on hook. Holding Blue to the back and working through **both** loops of **both** pieces, insert hook in any st on Rnd 3, YO and pull up a loop, slip st in each st around; cut yarn. Remove hook from loop. Insert hook from **back** to **front** through center of first st, hook loop and draw through, YO and pull end through loop.

SIDES & TOE

Rnd 1 (Right side)**:** With marked Sole away from you and working in Back Loops Only, join Blue with sc in marked loop *(see Joining With Sc, page 46)*; remove marker, sc in each st around; join with slip st to first sc: 32{36} sc.

Rnd 2: Ch 1, working in both loops, sc in same st as joining and in next 13{15} sc, hdc in next 4 sc, dc in next 8 sc, hdc in next 4 sc, sc in last 2{4} sc; join with slip st to first sc.

Rnd 3: Ch 1, sc in same st as joining, dc in next 10 sc, sc in next 3{5} sc, sc2tog twice, dc2tog 4 times, sc2tog twice, sc in last 2{4} sc; join with slip st to first sc: 24{28} sts.

Rnd 4: Ch 1, sc in same st as joining and in next 13{15} sts, dc2tog 4 times, sc in last 2{4} sc; join with slip st to first sc: 20{24} sts.

Rnd 5: Slip st in next 14{16} sc, sc in next dc, place marker in sc just made for Front Tab placement, sc in next 5 sts, slip st in last 0{2} sc *(see Zeros, page 45)*; finish off.

FRONT TAB

With **right** side facing, join Tan with slip st in marked sc, remove marker; ch 2, dc in same st and in next 4 sts, (dc, ch 2, slip st) in next st, leave remaining sts unworked; finish off.

LACES

With Off White, ch 25; finish off.

Using photo as a guide for placement, insert chain from **back** to **front** on Rnd 4, then back down on opposite side. Bring chain up on Rnd 3, then back down on opposite side and secure on the inside.

General Instructions

ABBREVIATIONS

BPdc	Back Post double crochet(s)
ch(s)	chain(s)
cm	centimeters
dc	double crochet(s)
dc2tog	double crochet 2 together
FPdc	Front Post double crochet(s)
hdc	half double crochet(s)
mm	millimeters
Rnd(s)	Round(s)
sc	single crochet(s)
sc2tog	single crochet 2 together
sc3tog	single crochet 3 together
sp(s)	space(s)
st(s)	stitch(es)
tr	treble crochet(s)
YO	yarn over

SYMBOLS & TERMS

★ — work instructions following ★ as many **more** times as indicated in addition to the first time.

( ) or **[ ]** — work enclosed instructions **as many** times as specified by the number immediately following **or** work all enclosed instructions in the stitch or space indicated **or** contains explanatory remarks.

colon (:) — the number(s) given after a colon at the end of a row or round denote(s) the number of stitches or spaces you should have on that row or round.

Yarn Weight Symbol & Names	LACE 0	SUPER FINE 1	FINE 2	LIGHT 3	MEDIUM 4	BULKY 5	SUPER BULKY 6	JUMBO 7
Type of Yarns in Category	Fingering, size 10 crochet thread	Sock, Fingering, Baby	Sport, Baby	DK, Light Worsted	Worsted, Afghan, Aran	Chunky, Craft, Rug	Super Bulky, Roving	Jumbo, Roving
Crochet Gauge* Ranges in Single Crochet to 4" (10 cm)	32-42 sts**	21-32 sts	16-20 sts	12-17 sts	11-14 sts	8-11 sts	6-9 sts	5 sts and fewer
Advised Hook Size Range	Steel*** 6 to 8, Regular hook B-1	B-1 to E-4	E-4 to 7	7 to I-9	I-9 to K-10½	K-10½ to M/N-13	M/N-13 to Q	Q and larger

*GUIDELINES ONLY: The chart above reflects the most commonly used gauges and hook sizes for specific yarn categories.

** Lace weight yarns are usually crocheted with larger hooks to create lacy openwork patterns. Accordingly, a gauge range is difficult to determine. Always follow the gauge stated in your pattern.

*** Steel crochet hooks are sized differently from regular hooks–the higher the number, the smaller the hook, which is the reverse of regular hook sizing.

GAUGE

Exact gauge is **essential** for proper fit. Before beginning your booties, make the Sole in the yarn and hook specified. After completing the Sole, measure it. If your piece is larger or smaller than specified, **make another, changing hook size to get the correct gauge**. Keep trying until you find the size hook that will give you the specified gauge.

MARKERS

Markers are used to help distinguish the beginning of each round being worked. Place a 2" (5 cm) scrap piece of yarn before the first stitch of each round, moving the marker after each round is complete.

When marking a stitch, use a split ring marker or a scrap piece of yarn.

ZEROS

To consolidate the length of a pattern, zeros are sometimes used so that both sizes can be combined. For example, slip st in last 0{2} sc means the first size would do nothing and the second size would slip st in last 2 sc.

CROCHET TERMINOLOGY		
UNITED STATES		INTERNATIONAL
slip stitch (slip st)	=	single crochet (sc)
single crochet (sc)	=	double crochet (dc)
half double crochet (hdc)	=	half treble crochet (htr)
double crochet (dc)	=	treble crochet (tr)
treble crochet (tr)	=	double treble crochet (dtr)
double treble crochet (dtr)	=	triple treble crochet (ttr)
triple treble crochet (tr tr)	=	quadruple treble crochet (qtr)
skip	=	miss

BEGINNER	Projects for first-time crocheters using basic stitches. Minimal shaping.
EASY	Projects using yarn with basic stitches, repetitive stitch patterns, simple color changes, and simple shaping and finishing.
INTERMEDIATE	Projects using a variety of techniques, such as basic lace patterns or color patterns, mid-level shaping and finishing.
EXPERIENCED	Projects with intricate stitch patterns, techniques and dimension, such as non-repeating patterns, multi-color techniques, fine threads, small hooks, detailed shaping and refined finishing.

CROCHET HOOKS																	
U.S.	B-1	C-2	D-3	E-4	F-5	G-6	7	H-8	I-9	J-10	K-10½	L-11	M/N-13	N/P-15	P/Q	Q	S
Metric - mm	2.25	2.75	3.25	3.5	3.75	4	4.5	5	5.5	6	6.5	8	9	10	15	16	19

JOINING WITH SC

When instructed to join with sc, begin with a slip knot on hook. Insert hook in stitch indicated, YO and pull up a loop, YO and draw through both loops on hook.

JOINING WITH DC

When instructed to join with dc, begin with a slip knot on hook. YO, holding loop on hook, insert hook in stitch indicated, YO and pull up a loop (3 loops on hook), (YO and draw through 2 loops on hook) twice.

BACK RIDGE

Work only in loops indicated by arrows ***(Fig. 1)***.

Fig. 1

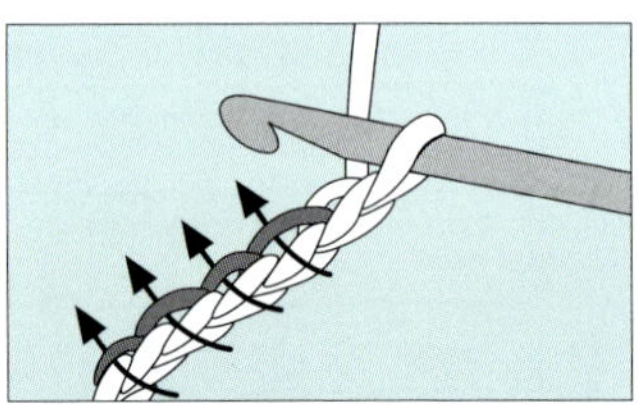

FREE LOOPS OF A CHAIN

When instructed to work in free loops of a chain, work in loop indicated by arrow ***(Fig. 2)***.

Fig. 2

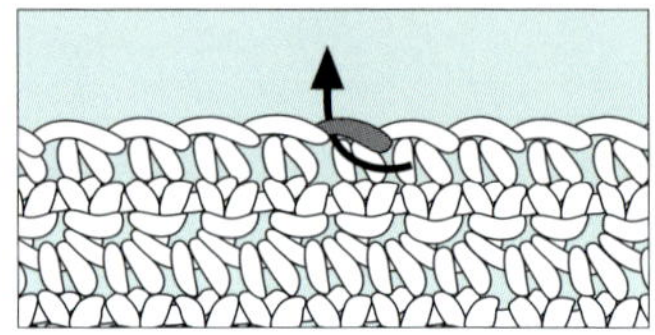

BACK OR FRONT LOOPS ONLY

Work only in loop(s) indicated by arrow ***(Fig. 3)***.

Fig. 3

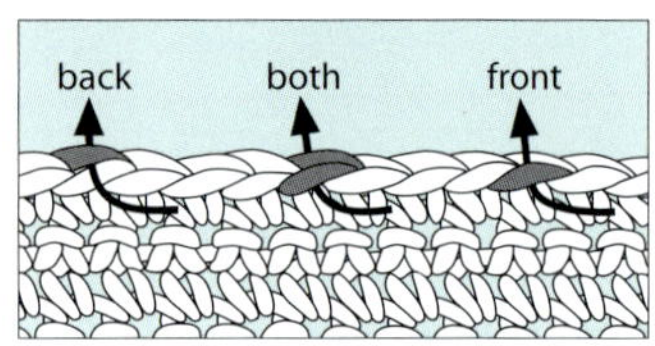

WORKING AROUND A STITCH

Work around stitch just made *(Fig. 4)*.

Fig. 4

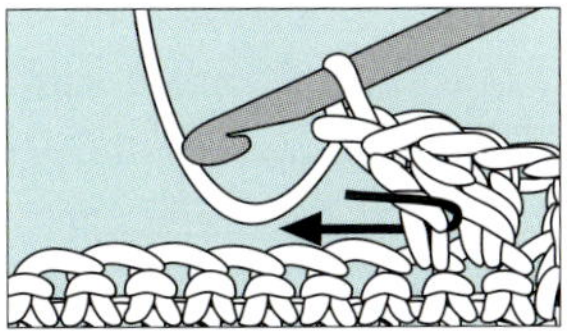

WORKING IN FRONT OF OR BEHIND A STITCH

Work in stitch indicated, inserting hook in direction of arrow *(Fig. 5a & b)*.

Fig. 5a

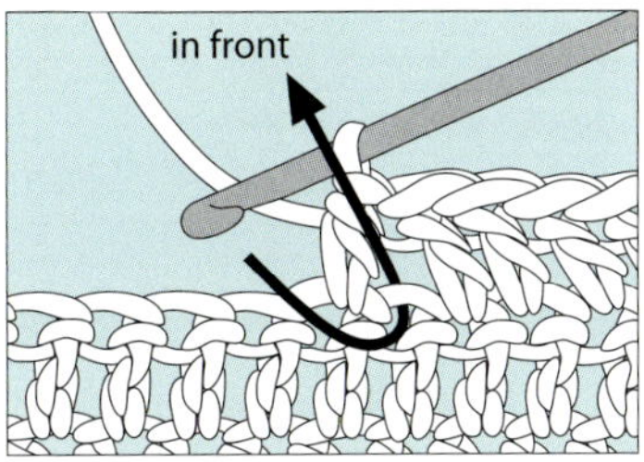

Fig. 5b

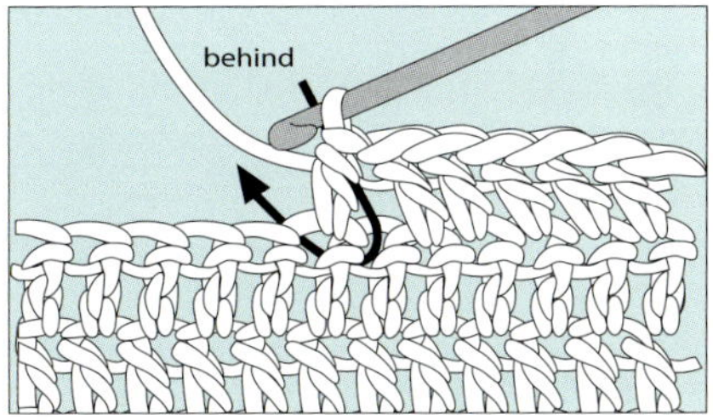

CHANGING COLORS

Drop yarn, insert hook in first stitch, with new yarn, YO and draw through stitch and loop on hook *(Fig. 6)*.

Fig. 6

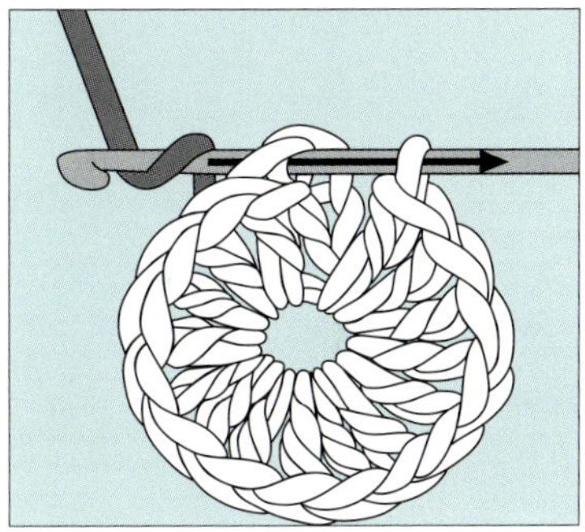

Yarn Information

The items in this book were made using medium weight yarn. Any brand of medium weight yarn may be used. Remember, to arrive at the finished size, it is the GAUGE/TENSION that is important, not the brand of yarn.

For your convenience, listed below are the yarns used to create our photography models. Because yarn manufacturers make frequent changes in their product lines, you may sometimes find it necessary to use a substitute yarn or to search for the discontinued product at alternate suppliers (locally or online).

CASUAL BOOTS
Caron® Simply Soft®
Green - #0003 Pistachio
Tan - #0008 Autumn Maize

CASUAL LOAFERS
Red Heart® Soft®
Ecru - #4601 Off White
Brown - #9344 Chocolate

MOTIF SANDALS
Caron® Simply Soft®
Pink - #9719 Soft Pink
Green - #0003 Pistachio

CROSSOVER SANDALS
Caron® Simply Soft®
Tan - #9703 Bone
Green - #9739 Soft Green

ESPADRILLES
Caron® Simply Soft®
Coral - #0015 Strawberry
Off White - #9702 Off White

FLOWER PETAL SLIPPERS
Caron® Simply Soft®
Yellow - #9755 Sunshine
White - #9701 White
Aqua - #9780 Robins Egg

HIGH-TOP MOCCASINS
Deborah Norville Collection Everyday® Soft Worsted
Ecru - #1002 Cream
Brown - #1014 Caramel
Aqua - #1017 Azure
Red - #1007 Really Red

HIGH-TOP SNEAKERS
Red Heart® Soft®
White - #4600 White
Blue - #9820 Mid Blue
Red - #9925 Really Red

LACY CUFF BOOTS
Red Heart® Soft Baby Steps®
Grey - #9401 Elephant
Lavender - #9590 Lavender
Caron® Simply Soft®
White - #9701 White
Pink - #9719 Soft Pink

PEEK-A-BOO SANDALS
Deborah Norville Collection Everyday® Soft Worsted
Orchid - #1032 Peony
Grey - #1023 Mist
Gold - #1028 Mustard

SPORTY SNEAKERS
Caron® Simply Soft®
Tan - #9703 Bone
Blue - #9712 Soft Blue
Off White - #9702 Off White

We have made every effort to ensure that these instructions are accurate and complete. We cannot, however, be responsible for human error, typographical mistakes, or variations in individual work.